LV

JUNE 28, 2013

Snap books®

Endangered and Threatened Animals

ORANGUTANS

by Janet Riehecky

Consultant:
Dean Gibson
Curator of Primates
San Diego Zoo Global
San Diego, California

CAPSTONE PRESS
a capstone imprint

Snap Books are published by Capstone Press,
1710 Roe Crest Drive, North Mankato, Minnesota 56003.
www.capstonepub.com

Library of Congress Cataloging-in-Publication Data
Riehecky, Janet, 1953-
  Orangutans / by Janet Riehecky.
     p. cm. – (Snap books: endangered and threatened animals)
  Includes bibliographical references and index.
  ISBN 978-1-4296-8587-0 (library binding)
  ISBN 978-1-62065-348-7 (ebook PDF)
  1. Orangutan—Juvenile literature. I. Title.
  QL737.P96R535 2013
  599.88'3—dc23
                         2012008522

Editor: Brenda Haugen
Designer: Bobbie Nuytten
Media Researcher: Marcie Spence
Production Specialist: Kathy McColley

Photo Credits:
Alamy: Paul Kingsley, 25, travelbild.com, 17 (top); AP Images: Milve.com, 28; Corbis: Binsar Bakkara/AP, 10, Luca Tettoni, 6, 23 (top); iStockphoto: Maxlevoyou, design element; Shutterstock: Agnes van der Logt, 4, A.S. Zain, 23 (middle), i359702, 7, Jan S., 18, Joseph Scott Photography, 13 (bottom), Kitch Bain, 21, margita, design element, Melissa Schalke, 9, Michael Rubin, cover, Nagel Photography, 13 (middle right), Peter Zachar, 23 (middle), Pics-xl, 17 (bottom), Tatiana Morozova, 19, Tischenko Irina, 23 (bottom), Tristan Tan, 26, Uryadnikov Sergey, 11, 13 (top and middle left), 15, 17 (middle), worldswildlifewonders, 14

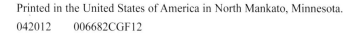

Printed in the United States of America in North Mankato, Minnesota.
042012   006682CGF12

Table of Contents

Chapter 1

In Danger

High in the rain forest trees, an orangutan swings from branch to branch. Her son clings to her back, his arms clasped tightly around her neck. Though he's almost 2 years old, he's never been away from his mother's side. During the next few years, he will rarely be out of his mother's sight. He will stay with her until he is about 8 years old. She will teach him everything he needs to know to live in the rain forest. He will learn what to eat, how to travel, and where to sleep. What his mother can't teach him is how to survive if the rain forest is destroyed. Many scientists believe that without help, orangutans will become **extinct** in the wild in the next 10 years.

extinct: no longer living; an extinct animal is one that has died out, with no more of its kind

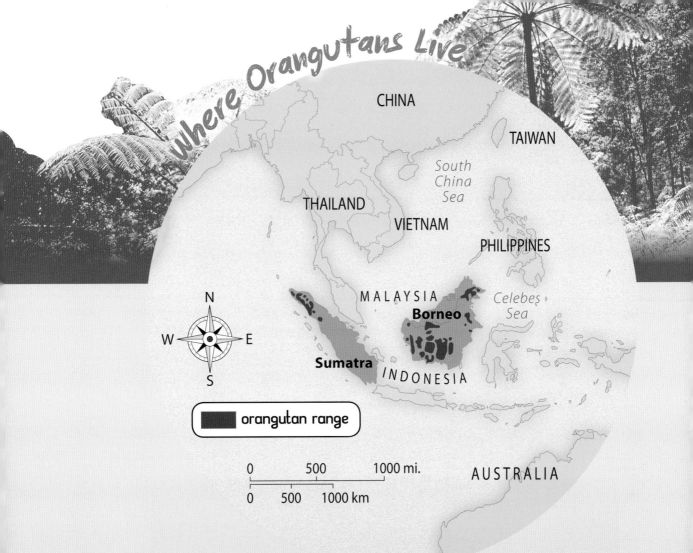

Orangutans live in the rain forests of Borneo and Sumatra in
Indonesia, in southeast Asia. These islands were once almost
covered with rain forests. Now there are only a few rain forests
on the two islands. More than half of the rain forest land on
Borneo is gone. Sumatra has lost 90 percent of the lowland
rain forest where orangutans live. Loggers have cut down rain
forest trees for their wood. Plantation owners have cleared
land to plant palm trees, which produce palm oil. This oil is
used as fuel and as an ingredient in many foods.

5

Orangutans could crowd together in the remaining rain forest, but there still wouldn't be enough food. An orangutan eats about 26 pounds (12 kilograms) of food each day. A 0.4 square mile (1 square kilometer) area of rain forest can only support one to three orangutans. Without enough food, the entire orangutan population is at risk.

Orangutans were first listed as **endangered** in 1970 by the International Union for Conservation of Nature (IUCN). Being listed as endangered means that an animal has a high risk of becoming extinct in the future.

Loss of rain forest habitat is one of the biggest threats to orangutans.

endangered: at risk of dying out

In 2000 the Sumatran orangutan's status changed to critically endangered. This means it has a high risk of becoming extinct in the near future. Being listed as endangered or critically endangered draws attention to the animal. But it doesn't mean anything will be done to help the animal. Governments and private groups need to help.

Because of their smaller population, Sumatran orangutans are at an even higher risk of extinction.

The loss of rain forest land has greatly reduced the orangutan population. Once orangutans numbered in the hundreds of thousands. But in 2009, scientists estimated that only about 60,000 orangutans were left. Each year there are fewer. Even under the best conditions, the orangutan population doesn't grow very fast. A female usually has only three or four babies during her lifetime.

About 900 orangutans live in zoos worldwide. But it's unlikely that these animals or their young could learn to live in the rain forests. They would not have the skills to find food. About 2,000 orangutans are currently being trained to live in the wild in **rehabilitation** camps in Sumatra and Borneo.

Orangutans are rarely predators or prey. Only tigers and clouded leopards are big enough to hunt orangutans, and these big cats are equally as rare. And though orangutans sometimes prey on small animals, orangutans eat mostly fruit and plants. But orangutans are an important part of the **ecosystem**. They help rain forests grow. The seeds they eat and spread around in their dung form new trees and plants.

rehabilitation: therapy that helps animals recover their health or abilities

ecosystem: a group of animals and plants that work together with their surroundings

Orangutans are not the only animals in their ecosystem that are in trouble. Thousands of other rain forest animals and plants could also be lost if their habitat is destroyed. Each plays an important part in the ecosystem.

Other Animals at Risk

Orangutans are not the only animals that are endangered in Borneo and Sumatra. Fewer than 1,000 pygmy elephants still roam Borneo. As few as 300 hairy rhinos remain in Sumatra. And fewer than 500 Sumatran tigers live on that island.

Loss of the rain forests is not the only reason orangutans are at risk. **Poachers** take baby orangutans to sell as pets. People sometimes kill orangutans for meat or out of fear. Wildfires have also killed hundreds of these animals. And when orangutans come in contact with people in the wild, they can catch human diseases. But there is hope.

Many people and groups are buying rain forest land to save it. And some people have opened rehabilitation camps in the rain forests. Orangutans that were poached and sold are rescued and taken to the camps. Camp staff teaches the animals the survival skills they weren't able to learn from their mothers. Most of these orangutans will be returned to the wild.

A staff member at a rehabilitation center in Sumatra watches a young orangutan play.

Meet Princess

Princess is an orangutan who got a second chance. She was poached as a baby and sold illegally as a pet. She was rescued when she was 2 or 3 years old. Princess was taken to Camp Leakey, a rehabilitation camp in Tanjung Puting National Park in Borneo. The camp staff trained Princess to live in the rain forest again. She learned how to find food and make a nest, but she also learned a few other things.

After watching people, Princess could paddle a canoe, wash clothes in the river, and unlock a door. She also learned 37 words in sign language and used them to communicate with people. She could ask for a drink of water or put two words together to identify "sweet fruit." She never fully **adapted** to a life in the wild, but she had five babies who did. Now in her late 30s, Princess still visits Camp Leakey. Rehabilitation camps such as Camp Leakey protect rain forest land. They also have helped hundreds of orangutans like Princess have a chance to live free.

poacher: a person who hunts or fishes illegally

adapt: to change to fit into a new or different environment

11

Chapter 2

Daily Life

Orangutans are the largest tree-dwelling animal in the world. They are the second largest **apes**, after gorillas. An average male orangutan grows almost 5 feet (1.5 meters) tall and weighs about 200 pounds (91 kg). Adult females are only about 3 feet (0.9 m) tall and weigh about 100 pounds (45 kg).

Orangutans have thick, heavy bodies covered with long red hair. Because they spend almost their entire lives in trees, their arms are longer and stronger than their legs. They can swing through the trees with ease and climb nearly flat surfaces. Their feet often act as a second pair of hands.

ape: a large primate with no tail

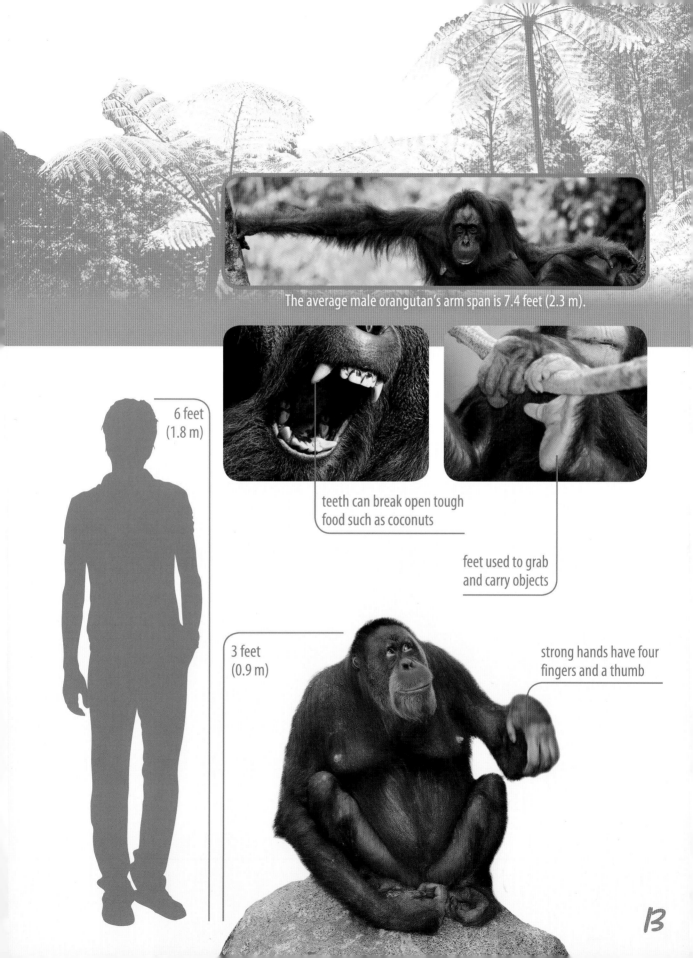

The average male orangutan's arm span is 7.4 feet (2.3 m).

6 feet
(1.8 m)

teeth can break open tough
food such as coconuts

feet used to grab
and carry objects

3 feet
(0.9 m)

strong hands have four
fingers and a thumb

13

Orangutans are strong animals with powerful hands. One researcher estimated that an orangutan is about seven times stronger than a man. An orangutan has a powerful grip and can hang from a tree branch for hours. An orangutan's hands are about the size of a catcher's mitt.

The biggest, toughest male usually **dominates** all the others in its **territory**. Called an alpha male, this orangutan grows large cheek pads and a throat pouch. These features make his head look bigger.

A male with large cheek pads and a throat pouch

The alpha male announces his presence with a long call. This cry starts with a low, soft grumble and builds into a roar. The cheek pads and throat pouch help make the cry very loud. The cry can be heard more than 1 mile (1.6 kilometers) away. The long call warns other males to stay away and invites females to visit the alpha male.

An alpha male roaring

Some scientists believe the long call also causes stress in young males. They think the stress keeps young males from growing large cheek pads and throat pouches. These features grow when the young males are big enough to challenge the alpha male. They also grow when the young males claim their own territories. Then they are alpha males too.

dominate: to have control over others
territory: an area of land that an animal claims as its own to live in

Orangutans travel from tree to tree, looking for food. Each night the animal stops traveling. It builds a big, comfortable nest made of branches and leaves where it sleeps. During hot afternoons, the animal often builds a nest for napping. It might add large leaves as a roof to provide shade.

Orangutans may travel together, depending on the food supply. If too many orangutans are in the same territory, there will not be enough food for all of them. Males travel through an area of about 4 to 5 square miles (10 to 13 square kilometers). Females cover a little more than half that space. If food is plentiful, several females may travel together.

Adult males and females do not live together except for a few weeks when mating. A female seeks a male when she is ready to mate. She mates only once every eight to 10 years. The male leaves within a few days of the female becoming pregnant. The female is pregnant for nine months. She usually gives birth to one baby in a nest high in the trees. A newborn orangutan weighs 3.3 to 4.4 pounds (1.5 to 2 kg).

Orangutan Life Cycle

- Infant orangutans stay with their mothers for their first two years.

- Between the ages of 2 and 5, orangutans wander short distances from their nests. They learn to gather food, though most orangutans still get milk from their mothers.

- Between the ages of 5 and 8, orangutans learn to be independent. They begin to travel alone and build nests. They also search for their own food.

- Around age 8, orangutans usually seek their own territories.

- Females mate for the first time around their 15th year.

- Wild orangutans can live into their 50s.

Orangutans eat more than 400 kinds of food. Their main food is fruit. They also eat nuts, leaves, flowers, insects, honey, bird eggs, and even spider webs. Orangutans get most of their water from juicy fruits. They also drink water from streams and water that collects in tree holes.

Orangutans have sharp memories and know every useful tree in their territories. An orangutan may notice a tree with its fruit only half ripe. The animal will return to the tree when the fruit is ripe. The animals also recognize and avoid poisonous plants.

Scientists believe orangutans use plants for other purposes. A researcher once saw an orangutan holding its head and looking miserable. The animal walked to a shrub and ate several handfuls of its flowers. About a half an hour later, the animal seemed fine. Orangutans have also been seen placing twigs from the *Campnospermum* tree in their nests. Its leaves are known to keep away mosquitoes.

Orangutans eat more than 300 kinds of fruit, including mangoes and figs.

Searching for Food

Orangutans spend up to six hours every day looking for food. About 90 percent of an orangutan's diet is fruit.

Amazing Orangutans

Chapter 3

Orangutans are quick learners. In zoos orangutans have watched their caretakers work. Some of these animals have learned to mix soap and water in a bucket and scrub their cage floors. Orangutans also copy actions such as chopping wood, painting, washing dishes, and brushing their teeth.

Orangutans can make and use tools. In the wild they use sticks to get honey from beehives. They also use sticks to remove the inner fruit from nuts. Orangutans turn leaves into umbrellas to protect themselves from the sun or rain. They also use leaves as gloves to protect their hands or to wipe their faces.

Orangutans have emotions and show happiness and sorrow. They also show that they care about others. A researcher visiting a Borneo rehabilitation camp sat with a sick orangutan. The researcher tried to feed the orangutan some blades of grass. Later the woman felt a tickle on her chin. The orangutan was offering her some grass.

Orangutans also remember people and events. A **captive** female orangutan was returned to the rain forest. On the day the animal was released, a male researcher took the orangutan into the jungle. He pulled a leaf from a shrub and gave it to the animal. Six years later the man returned to the rehabilitation camp, and the orangutan was visiting. The animal recognized the man, took him by the hand, and led him into the rain forest. The orangutan picked a leaf from the same type of shrub and gave it to him.

An orangutan's expressions and posture give clues to how it is feeling.

captive: kept in a cage

Chapter 4

Saving the Orangutan

In Borneo and Sumatra, scientists saw that the rain forest was being destroyed at an alarming rate. They knew orangutans could not survive this destruction. The Indonesian government set aside large areas of land as protected national forests. But some people ignore the law. They enter the forest and illegally chop down the trees. Nearly $3.4 billion worth of trees are illegally harvested each year. Organizations such as the Centre for Orangutan Protection try to stop these crimes. But illegal loggers are rarely caught. Only 10 percent of those caught ever go to court.

When orangutans lose their habitat, they use land claimed by people. They steal food, damage property, and may even hurt people. Some people shoot orangutans on sight, trying to protect themselves.

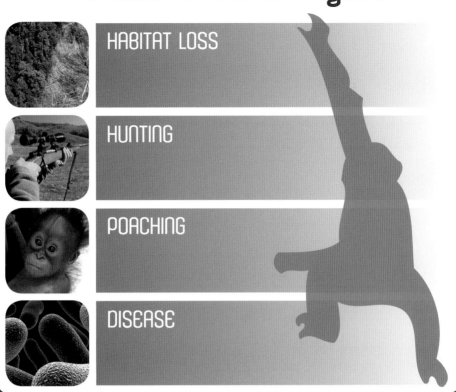

Threats to the Orangutan

- HABITAT LOSS
- HUNTING
- POACHING
- DISEASE

About 1,000 orangutans a year are killed or captured. Sometimes the orangutans are caught and used for entertainment, such as in boxing or wrestling matches. Small orangutans are sold as pets. Others are eaten.

Almost 3,000 orangutans have been rescued from captivity since 1970 by organizations such as the Sepilok Orangutan Rehabilitation Centre. But fewer than 12 people have gone to jail for removing these animals from the wild. Under the law, anyone who captures or injures protected animals can be punished by up to five years in jail. They also face fines of about $110. But the actual sentences are usually much lighter.

One of the most successful efforts to help orangutans is happening in Samboja Lestari in Borneo. This small town was once in the middle of the rain forest. In the 1950s a corporation began cutting down the trees. When most of the trees were gone, the water sources became polluted. The ground was too poor to grow crops. The corporation left, and there was no more work for the villagers. Huge fires in 1997 and 1998 made the situation worse. Thick smoke polluted the atmosphere and water sources dried up. The flames killed people and animals and destroyed the few trees that were left.

In 2001 the Borneo Orangutan Survival Foundation (BOS) began buying land around Samboja Lestari. They wanted to restore the rain forest and provide a place for orangutans to live. They hired villagers to fertilize the land and grow trees.

By 2005 BOS owned 4,300 acres (1,740 hectares) of land and had planted 800,000 trees. They also planted fruits and vegetables among the trees, for both orangutans and people. BOS hired villagers to provide security, do construction work, and care for about 200 orangutans. This land is now a prosperous village and a **sanctuary** for orangutans and many other animals. BOS continues to plant more trees and help rehabilitate orangutans.

A Helping Hand

In Samboja Lestari, some orangutans receive help on a series of islands. When a rescued orangutan has a disability, the animal is moved to one of these islands. There the animal gets help so it can live a natural lifestyle. Food is provided for the orangutans, but they also find some food for themselves. They learn to climb trees and build nests.

Feeding time at a rehabilitation center in Borneo

sanctuary: a place where animals are cared for and protected

Chapter 5

You Can Help

One way to help save orangutans is to learn more about them and the issues they face. Then share that information with others. You can write letters to government officials and corporations that destroy rain forests. Or you can write articles for a blog or newspaper. When you are done, ask your friends to write too.

Another way to help is not to buy things made from rain forest wood or palm oil. One of the main reasons orangutan habitat is cleared is to grow oil palms. The oil from the fruit and kernels is used in many food products, such as margarine, cooking oil, baked goods, and candy. Check product labels to see if palm oil is used.

palm oil and kernels

Another way to help is to support groups that help orangutans. Organizations that work to save orangutans always need money. You could hold a fund-raiser, such as a bake sale or car wash, to make some money. You could also host an endangered species fair. You could set up booths and sell handmade items or play games. The Orangutan Foundation International will let you become a foster parent to one of their orangutans.

Sometimes you can also donate your time if you live near a zoo. Teen artist Pearce Thompson visited the Chauffee Zoological Gardens in Fresno, California. He saw the orangutans were bored in their cages, so he tried to help one of them. Pearce painted scenes on large rolls of paper to put in one orangutan's cage to entertain the animal.

Two young girls have been working to help save orangutans. Girl Scouts Rhiannon Tomtishen and Madison Vorva learned that the cookies they were selling contained palm oil. Rhiannon and Madison wanted the Girl Scouts to use canola oil or some other oil in their cookies. This change would help save rain forest land for orangutans and other animals.

They contacted an executive at the Girl Scouts. In 2008 Girl Scout officials agreed to look into alternatives to Southeast Asian palm oil. By 2015, this palm oil will no longer be used in the cookies. In 2012, the **United Nations** named the girls Forest Heroes for their efforts.

Girl Scouts Rhiannon Tomtishen (left) and Madison Vorva

Orangutans Online

There are lots of Web sites that have information about orangutans. Look up the places below, and then share what you've learned.

- **National Geographic Kids** has orangutan-related games, pictures, and facts. See one of these animals swinging through the trees. Watch a video of a female orangutan and her young in the wild. Send an orangutan e-card to a friend.

- **The San Diego Zoo** has information about orangutans. Check out the orangutan photos and watch a video of an orangutan's birthday party. Learn about the zoo's most famous orangutan, Ken Allen. You can even buy art made by one of these amazing animals!

- **The World Wildlife Fund** is the world's leading conservation group. Learn more about the threats orangutans face and how you can help. You can even adopt an orangutan.

The possibilities for helping orangutans are endless. Using your imagination, you might be able to come up with some great ideas of your own too.

United Nations: a group of countries that works together for peace and security

Glossary

adapt (uh-DAPT)—to change to fit into a new or different environment

ape (APE)—a large primate with no tail; gorillas, orangutans, and chimpanzees are kinds of apes

captive (KAP-tiv)—kept in a cage

dominate (DAH-muh-nayt)—to have control over others

ecosystem (EE-koh-sis-tuhm)—a group of animals and plants that work together with their surroundings

endangered (in-DAYN-juhrd)—at risk of dying out

extinct (ik-STINGKT)—no longer living; an extinct animal is one that has died out, with no more of its kind

habitat (HAB-uh-tat)—the natural place and conditions in which an animal or plant lives

poacher (POHCH-ur)—a person who hunts or fishes illegally

rain forest (RAYN FOR-ist)—a warm area where many trees and plants grow closely together because of heavy rainfall

rehabilitation (ree-huh-bil-uh-TAY-shun)—therapy that helps animals recover their health or abilities

sanctuary (SANGK-choo-ayr-ee)—a place where animals are cared for and protected

territory (TER-uh-tor-ee)—an area of land that an animal claims as its own to live in

United Nations (yoo-NI-ted NAY-shuns)—a group of countries that works together for peace and security

Read More

Hunter, Rebecca. *Rain Forests*. Eco Alert. Mankato, Minn.: Sea-to-Sea Publications, 2012.

Laman, Tim, and Cheryl Knott. *Face to Face with Orangutans*. Washington, D.C.: National Geographic, 2009.

Newland, Sonya. *Rain Forest Animals*. Saving Wildlife. Mankato, Minn.: Smart Apple Media, 2012.

Silverman, Buffy. *Orangutans*. Living in the Wild. Primates. Chicago: Heinemann Library, 2012.

Internet Sites

FactHound offers a safe, fun way to find Internet sites related to this book. All of the sites on FactHound have been researched by our staff.

Here's all you do:

Visit *www.facthound.com*

Type in this code: 9781429685870

Check out projects, games and lots more at
www.capstonekids.com

Index